VICTORIAN
JINGLES

VICTORIAN JINGLES

COLLECTED BY DOROTHY BAKER

DRAWINGS BY JAMES DOLBY

Some of the Jingles in this book were current before Victorian times but are included because they were still current at that time, and many of these are still in use. Many of the Jingles have several versions — in these cases the version commonest in Victorian times has been used.

Published by
Thornhill Press Ltd.
46 Westgate Street
Gloucester

© *Dorothy Baker and James Dolby 1976*

ISBN 0 904110 27 3

Produced by
Oxford Publishing Company
Printed by
S & S Press, Abingdon

Button to chin till May comes in,
Ne'er cast a clout till May be out.

*

No buds, no bees,
No leaves on the trees,
No sun to shine,
No...vember.

*

If Candlemass day be warm and bright,
Winter will take another bite;
But if Candlemass brings cold and rain,
Winter is gone and won't come again.

*

Whether the weather be fine,
Whether the weather be not,
Whether the weather be cold,
Whether the weather be hot,
We'll weather the weather,
Whatever the whether,
Whether we like it or not.

*

When November's ice will bear a duck,
Winter will be all slosh and muck.

*

When the wind is in the east
Tis neither good for man nor beast;
When the wind is in the north
The prudent angler goes not forth;
When the wind is in the south
It blows the bait from the fishes mouth;
But when the wind is in the west,
Then the wind's by far the best.

*

He who in January sows oats,
Gets gold and groats;
He who sows them in May,
Gets little that way.

*

In March
the birds begin to search;
In April
the corn begins to fill;
In May
the birds begin to lay.

*

Evening red and morning grey
Help the traveller on his way;
Evening grey and morning red
Bring down rain upon his head.

*

April weather,
Rain and sunshine
Both together.

*

When you hear the asses bray,
We shall have some rain that day.

*

Barnaby bright,
Longest day,
Shortest night.

*

In March the cuckoo starts,
In April tunes his bill,
In May he sings all day,
In June he changes his tune,
In July he flies away.

*

If the moon shows a silver shield
Be not afraid to reap the field,
But if she rises haloed round,
Soon we'll tread on deluged ground.

*

4

Red skies at night,
A shepherd's delight;
Red skies at morning,
A shepherd's warning.

*

April showers bring forth May flowers,
A wet and windy May fills the barn with hay,
But a stormy September, then a winter nobody wants to
                                        remember.

*

A green Christmas makes a full churchyard.

*

On Swithin's Day if it doth rain,
For forty days it will remain
But if St. Swithin's day be fair,
For forty days t'will rain no more.

*

Remember on St. Vincent's Day,
If the sun his rays display,
Be sure to mark the transient beam
Which through the casement sheds a gleam,
For'tis a token bright and clear
Of prosperous weather all the year.

*

Mackerel backs and mare's tails,
Make tall ships carry short sails.

*

A swarm of bees in May
Is worth a load of hay;
A swarm of bees in June
Is worth a silver spoon;
But a swarm of bees in July
Isn't worth a fly.

*

Rain before seven,
Shine before eleven.

*

Fog on the hill,
Water for the Mill;
Fog in the hollow,
A fine day will follow.

*

March wind and May sun,
Make clothes white and maidens dun.

*

Long foretold, long last;
Short warning, soon past.

*

If you look at your corn in May,
You'll come weeping away;
If you look at your corn in June
You'll come home to another tune.

*

Many haws, many snows.

*

A peck of March dust
And a shower in May,
Make the corn green
And the fields gay.

*

Many frosts and many snows make rotten yowes (ewes)

*

Oak before the ash,
Summer will be a splash;
Ash before the oak,
Summer will be a soak.

❖

Mackerel sky, never long dry.

*

Rainbow at morn,
Put your hook in the corn;
Rainbow at eve,
Put your head in the sheave.

*

If the robin sings in the bush
The weather will be coarse;
But if the robin sings in the barn
The weather will be warm.

*

A dry May and a dripping June
Bring all things in tune.

*

If the cock moults before the hen
The weather will be thick and thin;
But if the hen moults before the cock
The weather will be hard as rock.

*

If the cock crows on going to bed
He's sure to rise with a watery head.

*

Rain from the east, wet two days at least.

*

COUNTRY LORE

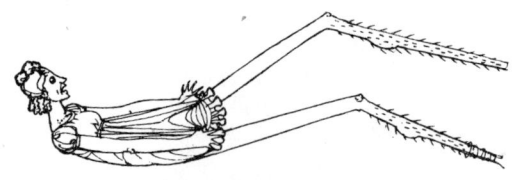

A lie has long legs.

*

Crafty men condemn studies,
Simple men admire them,
Wise men use them.

*

A pound of pluck is worth a ton of luck.

*

Poverty is want of much,
Avarice of everything.

*

Plough deep while sluggards sleep,
And you'll have corn to sell or keep.

*

Wash on Monday, best day.
Wash on Tuesday, slight delay.
Wash on Wednesday, no great blame.
Wash on Thursday, wash for shame.
Wash on Friday, wash in need.
Wash on Saturday, slut indeed.

*

Apple tart without the cheese,
Is like a kiss without the squeeze.

*

One for sorrow,
Two for joy,
Three for a girl,
Four for a boy,
Five for silver,
Six for gold,
And seven for a secret that must never be told.
(Magpie warning)

*

You can't go through a wood,
And through a wood,
Without picking up
A crooked stick.

*

The secret of two, no further will go.
The secret of three, a hundred will know.

*

Time flies, you say?,
No, no,
Time stays,
You go.

*

Cold water is the best of drinks,
So prophets, sages say.
Let princes revel at the pump,
And poets debauch on tea,
But whisky, wine and even beer,
Are good enough for me.

*

Happy is the bride whom the sun shines on,
Blessed is the corpse that the rain rains on.

*

A son is a son till he gets him a wife,
A daughter's a daughter the rest of your life.

*

Parsley won't grow where the missus is master

*

Harry no man's cattle.

*

I wander north, I wander south, I rest where'er I please.
See how the river banks are whipped, beneath the
*   autumn breeze,*
Yet what care I if autumn blasts the river banks lay bare.
The loss of green to the river banks is the river banks'
*   affair.*

*

Some go to church to see and be seen,
Some go there to say they have been,
Some go there to sleep and nod,
But few go there to worship God.

*

He who bathes in May,
Will soon be laid in clay;
He who bathes in June
Will sing a merry tune:
He who bathes in July
Will dance until he's dry.

*

If beards were all, the goat could preach.

*

After a famine in the stall
Comes a famine in the hall.

You can eat an apple, an egg or a nut,
Even though they be dressed by a slut.

*

If the adder could hear
And the blindworm see,
Neither man nor beast
Would ever go free.

*

It's an ill bred dog that bites a bitch.

*

In the Church's field of battle,
In its warfare and its strife,
You will find the Christian soldier,
Represented by his wife.

*

Let the wealthy and great,
Roll in splendour and state.
I envy them not, I declare it.
I eat my own lamb, my own chicken and ham,
I sheer my own fleece, and I wear it.
I have fruit, I have flowers,
I have lawns, I have bowers,
The lark is my morning alarming.
So jolly boys now,
Here's God-speed to the plough,
Long life and success to all farming.
                    (Harvest song.)

*

Friends, but not too friendly.
Neighbours, but not too neighbourly.
                    (Dorset saying.)

*

Early to bed, early to rise,
Makes a man healthy, wealthy and wise.

*

Live well, die never. Die well, live forever.

*

Thirty days hath September,
April, June and November,
All the rest have thirty one,
Excepting February with twenty eight,
But leap year coming once in four,
Brings poor February one day more.
                    *

Grass doesn't grow on a busy street.

The crab of the wood, is sauce very good
To serve with the crab of the sea;
But the wood of the crab is sauce for the drab
Who won't with her mistress agree.

*

Look to the cow, the sow, the mow,
And all will then be well enow.

*

A cherry year, a merry year,
A plum year, a dumb year.

*

Cheshire born and Cheshire bred,
Strong i'th'arm and thick i'th'head.

*

Ingleborough, Pendle and Penyghent,
Are the highest hills between Tweed and Trent.

*

He that buys land may buy many stones;
He that buys meat may buy many bones;
He that buys eggs buys many shells;
But he that buys ale buys nothing else.

*

Calf love, half love; old love, cold love.

*

Young men look forward,
Old men look backward,
The middle-aged look around.

*

A spider in the morning sorrow brings,
At evening dusk, good luck to you he sings.

*

Think of me in the hour of pleasure,
Think of me in the hour of leisure,
And if forgotten in the hour of care,
Think of me in the hour of prayer

*

What is it that a miser spends,
A spendthrift saves,
A rich man wants,
And all men carry to their graves?
NOTHING.

*

If you meet a piebald pony,
Wish before you see his tail.

*

Two things never seen,
A satisfied farmer or a dead donkey.

*

A housewife sweet, a kitchen neat,
There you can find good things to eat.

*

Hospitality polishes the pots.

*

See a pin and pick it up,
All the day you'll have good luck.
See a pin and let it lie,
You'll want a pin before you die.

*

An hour in the morning
Is worth two in the afternoon.

*

Kissing's out of fashion
When the gorse is out of bloom

*

In my young days:
It was man to the plough, girl to the sow,
Wife to the cow, boy to the mow.

Now it is:
Man tally-ho girl pian-oh, ,
Wife silk and satin, boy Greek and Latin.
                    (A Hampshire farmer.)

*

Dearly beloved brethren is it not a sin,
When you peel potatoes to throw away the skin?
Skin feeds pigs,
Pigs feed you;
Dearly beloved brethren is this not true?

*

The Five Alls

The King reigns over all.

The lawyer pleads for all.
The parson prays for all.

The soldier fights for all.

The ploughman pays for all.

*

Please to remember
The fifth of November,
Gunpowder treason and plot;
I see no reason
Why gunpowder treason
Should ever be forgot.

*

The Devil was sick,
The Devil a monk would be;
The Devil was well,
The Devil a monk was he.

*

He that agrees against his will
Is of his own opinion still.

*

Cobblers and tinkers
Are the best drinkers.

*

Pride breakfasts with plenty,
Dines with poverty,
Sups with infamy.

*

Old church, new steeple,
Poor parish, proud people.

*

The smaller the peas,
The more to the pot;
The fairer the woman,
The more the giglot.

*

For the sake of a nail the shoe was lost,
For the sake of a shoe the horse was lost,
For the sake of a horse the rider was lost,
For the sake of a rider the message was lost,
For the sake of a message the battle was lost,
For the sake of a battle the war was lost,
For the sake of a war the crown was lost;
And all for the sake of a horse-shoe nail.

*

Yellow forget and green forswear,
Red and blue are lucky to wear.

*

The law doth punish man or woman
That steals the goose from off the common,
But lets the greater felon loose
That steals the common from the goose.

*

Hark, hark, the dogs do bark,
The beggars are coming to town,
Some in rags and some in tags
And one in a velvet gown.

*

Feed a cold and starve a fever.

*

Half a pound of tuppenny rice,
Half a pound of treacle,
Mix it up and make it nice,
Pop goes the weasel.

Up and down the City Road,
In and out the Eagle,
That's the way the world goes round,
Pop goes the weasel.

Every time that I go out
The monkey's on the table,
Get a stick and knock if off,
Pop goes the weasel.

*

There were three jovial huntsmen,
A hunting they would go,
Up the hills and down the dales
Calling . . . Tally ho.

They hunted and they halloed,
But the first thing they did find
Was a fat pig lying in a ditch,
So this they left behind.

One said it was a fat pig,
But another, he said 'Nay,
It's just a London alderman
Whose clothes are stole away.'

*

The drink of true democracy
And free from all hypocrisy,
Alike to aristocracy
And every common man.
It adds to jocularity,
Enjoys a popularity,
It spares a drop for charity
And cheers the heart of man . . . Beer.

*

When horses are horses, to ride and to race,
Then women and wine, take a second place,
For me .. for me ... for me .... for me.

*

If you lose, say nothing;
If you win, say less.

*

For the food we eat
And those who prepare it,
For health to enjoy it
And for friends to share it,
We thank Thee O Lord

*

Shall we emulate the fishes, those wise little fishes, who
drink a great deal and say nothing?

*

Four of sour,
Two of sweet,
Three of strong
And four of weak.
(Rum Punch)

*

All men's servant, yet no man's slave.

*

He who has an art
Has everywhere a part.

*

Little children and fools
Should never play
With sharp edged tools.

*

The written word may long remain
Write no word that giveth pain.

*

Some have health and no wealth,
Some wealth and no health,
Some have health and wealth,
And some have neither health nor wealth.

*

Those who dance are thought mad by those who can't
hear the music.

*

Don't put your hand by hazard in the creel,
You may take out an adder or an eel.

*

Christmas is coming, the goose is getting fat,
Please put a penny in the old man's hat;
If you haven't got a penny, a ha'penny will do,
If you haven't got a ha'penny, God bless you.

*

A whistling woman and a crowing hen,
Are neither good to gods nor men.

*

Patience is a virtue,
Find it where you can,
Seldom in a woman,
Never in a man.

*

If Ifs and Ands were pots and pans,
And little pigs had wings,
Then nobody need pay to ride
And beggars would be kings.

*

I wish I were a bobby,
All dressed in bobby's clothes,
With a tall top hat
And a belt full of fat
And whiskers round my nose.

*

Little Miss Muffet across the way,
Fainted in her bath one day;
The neighbours didn't know what to say
So they went and fetched a policeman.

*

I paints and paints
With no complaints
And sells before they're dry;
Along comes Ruskin
And puts his tusk in,
Now nobody will buy.
    (Cry of a Victorian painter)

*

I've been asked to go,
I've been asked to go,
My daughter's going as Lady Godiva,
I wouldn't miss the sight for a fiver;
My wife's going to go
As cupid with a bow,
She'll be there with her bandy legs
And I've been asked to go.
                (Pierrot Song)

*

Hard up, hard up, a-knocking on thi door;
Nowt to lend,
Nowt to spend,
Things is getting waur;
Jobs all stop,
Clothes in pop,
Nowt t' eat but grass;
Tha's got t' be a beggar when tha's reight baht brass.

*

An ape's an ape
And a varlet's a varlet,
Though they be clad
In silk and in scarlet.

*

For every evil under the sun,
There is a remedy or there's none;
If there is one try to find it
If there's none, never mind it

*

After having your fling,
Look out for the sting.

*

When everybody's somebody, nobody's anybody.

*

Three times a bridesmaid,
Never a bride.

*

Change the name,
And not the letter,
You change for worse,
And not for better.

*

Married in white,
Sure to be right;
Married in green,
Sorrow is seen;
Married in yellow,
Ashamed of the fellow.

*

A bride must wear. . . .
Something old,
Something new,
Something borrowed,
And something blue.

*

Marry in haste, repent at leisure.

*

In marriage there are five bears:
Bear, and forbear.

*

This won't do,
To be married tomorrow,
The man to find
And the money to borrow.

*

Tinker, tailor,
Soldier, sailor,
Ploughboy,
Apothecary,
Thief.

*

There's always one who loves,
And one who is loved.

*

The marriage ceremony;
Aisle,
Altar,
Hymn.

*

When the husband drinks to the wife,
He would all were well.
When the wife drinks to the husband,
All is well.

*

Lad's love is lass's delight,
If lads won't love, lasses will flite. (Scold)

*

Honest men marry soon, wise men never.

*

A maid oft seen, or a gown oft worn,
Are not esteemed but held in scorn.

*

Haste makes waste,
Waste makes want,
Want makes strife,
Between husband and wife.

*

Maids want nothing but husbands, and when they have
husbands want everything.

*

Keep your eyes open before marriage and half shut after.

*

Pursue love and it will flee thee,
Flee love, it will pursue thee.

*

Married in January's hoar and rime,
Widowed you'll be before your time;

Married in February's sleety weather,
Life in time you'll tread together;

Married in March when winds shrill and roar,
Your home will lie on a foreign shore;

Married 'neath April's cheerful skies,
A chequered path before you lies;

Married in May when bees o'er blossoms flit,
Strangers around your board will sit;

Married in month of roses, June,
Your life will be a long honeymoon;

Married in July's heat and blaze,
Bitter-sweet memories will come of former days;

Married in August's warmth and drowse,
Lover and friend is your chosen spouse;

Married in September's golden glow,
Smooth and serene your life will flow;

Married when leaves in October thin,
Toil and hardship for you begin;

Married in November's icy blast,
Midst strangers' paths your lot is cast;

Married in December's foggy mist,
Dame fortune your wedding ring has kissed.

*

Oh, soldier, soldier will you marry me, with your musket,
                                        fife and drum?
Oh no, my pretty maid, I cannot marry you for I have
                                        no shirt to put on.
So she went upstairs to her father's chest.
And she brought him a  *of the very, very, best,*
And the soldier put it on.

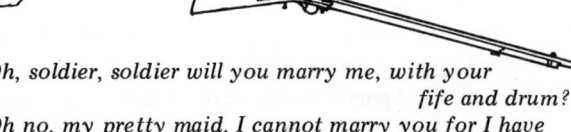

Oh, soldier, soldier will you marry me, with your
                                        fife and drum?
Oh no, my pretty maid, I cannot marry you for I have
                                        no coat to put on.
So she went upstairs to her father's chest,
And she brought him a of the very, very, best,
And the soldier put it on.

Oh, soldier, soldier will you marry me, with your musket,  and drum?

Oh no, my pretty maid, I cannot marry you for I have no boots to put on.

So she went upstairs to her father's chest,
And she brought him the 👢 of the very, very best,

And the soldier put them on.

Oh, soldier, soldier will you marry me, with your musket, fife and 🥁 ?

Oh no, my pretty maid, I cannot marry you, for I have a wife at home.

To furnish a ship requireth much trouble;
To furnish a woman, the charges are double.

*

If you carry a nutmeg in your pocket,
You'll be married to an old man.

*

The first month is honeymoon snick snack,
The second all hither and thither,
The third one thwick and thwack,
The fourth? — the devil take them
That brought thee and I together.

*

He that would the daughter win
Must with the mother first begin.

*

Drive the devil into a wife and you'll never drive him
                                                    out again.

*

Before you marry
Be sure of a house
Wherein to tarry.

*

Lazy wives break an arm at the church door.

*

Who made my bath much, much too hot,
Who slapped me in my little cot,
And when I cried, cared not one jot?
My mother !!!

*

You must not throw upon the floor
The crust you cannot eat,
For many a hungry little one
Would think it quite a treat.

*

In time, take time, when time does last,
For time is no time, when time is past.

*

Let's to bed, said Sleepy Head,
Tarry a while, said Slow,
Put on the pan, cried Greedy Nan,
Let's sup before we go.

*

Two legs sat on three legs,
One leg on his lap;
In came four legs,
Ran away with one leg,
Up jumped two legs,
Picked up three legs,
Threw it after four legs
And made him bring back one leg

*

Ladybird, ladybird, fly away home,
Your house is on fire and your children all gone.

*

To market, to market,
To buy a fat pig;
Home again, home again,
Jiggety jig.

*

Mother may I go and bathe?
Yes my darling daughter,
Hang your clothes upon a tree
But don't go near the water.

*

There was an old crow sat on a clod,
That's the end of my song; that's odd.

*

Monday's child is fair of face,

Tuesday's child is full of grace;

Wednesday's child is full of woe,

Thursday's child has far to go;

Friday's child is loving and giving,

Saturday's child must work for his living;

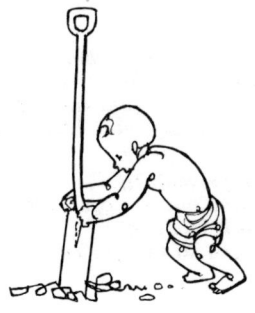

And the child that is born on the Sabbath Day,
Is merry and happy and bright and gay.

*

Three little mice sat down to spin,
Pussy passed by and she looked in,
"Shall I come in and bite your threads off?"
"Oh no thank you, Pussy, you'll bite our heads off."

*

What are little boys made of?
Slugs and snails and puppy dogs' tails . . .
What are little girls made of?
Sugar and spice and all things nice.

*

This little pig went to market.
This little pig stayed at home.
This little pig had roast beef.
This little pig had none.
And this little pig went oh, oh, oh,
All the way home.

*

My mother said, I never should
Play with the gipsies in the wood;
If I did, she would say:
Such a naughty girl as this
Is sure to run astray.

*

Adam and Eve and Pinchme
Went down to the water to bathe;
Adam and Eve were drowned,
So who do you think was saved?

*

I saw Esau kissing Kate,
The fact is, we all three saw,
For I saw Esau, he saw me,
And she saw I saw Esau.

*

Hungry dogs eat dirty puddings.

*

There was an old woman, As I heard tell,
Who went to the market her eggs for to sell;
She went to market all on a market day,
But she fell asleep on the King's highway.

By came a peddlar whose name was Stout,
And he cut her petticoats all round about,
He cut off her petticoats up to her knees,
Which made the old woman to shiver and sneeze.

When the old woman at last did wake,
She began to tremble and she began to shake;
She began to quiver, and she began to cry:
"Lord a-mercy on us, this is none of I,

But if it be I, as I hope it will be,
I've a little dog at home and he'll know me.
If it be I, he'll wag his little tail,
And if it be not, he'll loudly bark and wail."

Home went the little woman, all in the dark,
Up jumped the little dog and he began to bark;
He began to bark and she began to cry:
"Lord a-mercy on us, this is none of I."

*

Never trouble trouble till trouble troubles you,
You'll only double trouble,
And trouble others too.

*

Jack Sprat could eat no fat,
His wife could eat no lean,
And so between the pair of them
They licked the platter clean.

*

Hot cross buns, hot cross buns,

If your daughters don't like them

Give them to your sons;

Two a penny,

Three a penny,

HOT, CROSS, BUNS.

*

Roses are red,
Violets are blue,
Honey is sweet
And so are you.

*

Winifred Willis,
Wilfully wasted
What was wanted,
When we were without
Woman's wonderful wisdom.

*

Brothers and sisters have I none,
But that man's father is my father's son.
Who is that man?

*

Nature needs five hours of sleep,
Custom gives seven,
Laziness takes nine,
And wickedness eleven.

*

A window has a little pain,
And so have I;
The window's pain is in its sash,
I wonder why?

*

Cross patch draw the latch,
Sit by the fire and spin;
Take a cup, and drink it up,
Then call the neighbours in.

*

Dance a baby didit,
What shall a mother do widit?
Sit it on lap,
And give it some pap,
Then dance a baby didit.

*

Two little birdies sat on a wall,
One called Peter, one called Paul;
Fly away Peter, fly away Paul;
Come back Peter, come back Paul.

*

Look after the pence,
And the pounds will look after themselves.

*

Pudding time comes once a day;
When the meat is cleared away,
We all turn round and look to see
What the pudding's going to be.
We clap our hands if up there comes
A lovely pudding stuffed with plums;
But wholesome things like treacle, rice,
We do not think so very nice.

*

Matilda ate jam,
Matilda ate jelly;
Matilda went home with a pain in her . . . . .
Now don't get excited,
Now don't be misled,
Matilda went home with a pain in her head.

*

Good, better, best, never let it rest,
Till your better's better, and your better's best.

*

Four posts round my bed,
Four angels guard my head,
Matthew, Mark, Luke and John,
Bless the bed that I lie on.

*

When little birds within their nest agree,
I think it is a shameful sight,
For members of a family,
To quarrel and to fight.

*

If the wind changes,
Your cross face will stay,
So smile and look pleasant
Throughout the long day.

*

Wilful waste makes woeful want,
So you may live to say . . .
Oh how I wish I had the crust,
That once I threw away.

*

Satan finds work in plenty
For idle hands to do.

*

Charlie, Charlie, chuck chuck chuck,
Tried to swim like a little duck;
Poor Charlie died,
The little duck cried
Quack quack, Charlie, chuck chuck chuck.

*

Jeremiah, blow the fire,
Puff puff puff;
First you blow it gently,
Then you blow it rough.

*

One two, buckle my shoe.
Three four, knock at the door.
Five six, pick up sticks,
Seven eight, lay them straight.
Nine ten, a good fat hen.
Eleven twelve, dig and delve.
Thirteen fourteen, maids a-courting.
Fifteen sixteen, maids a-fixt-in.
Nineteen twenty, my plate's empty.

*

I'll tell you a story
About Jack-a-Nory,
And now my story's begun;
I'll tell you another
About Jack and his brother
And now my story is done.

*   *